THE BLOCKADE RUNNERS

THE BLOCKADE RUNNERS

Jules Verne

TABLE OF CONTENTS

THE DOLPHIN

The Clyde was the first river whose waters were lashed into foam by a steam-boat. It was in 1812 when the steamer called the Comet ran between Glasgow and Greenock, at the speed of six miles an hour. Since that time more than a million of steamers or packet-boats have plied this Scotch river, and the inhabitants of Glasgow must be as familiar as any people with the wonders of steam navigation.

However, on the 3rd of December, 1862, an immense crowd, composed of shipowners, merchants, manufacturers, workmen, sailors, women, and children, thronged the muddy streets of Glasgow, all going in the direction of Kelvin Dock, the large shipbuilding premises belonging to Messrs. Tod & MacGregor. This last name especially proves that the descendants of the famous Highlanders have become manufacturers, and that they have made workmen of all the vassals of the old clan chieftains.

Kelvin Dock is situated a few minutes' walk from the town, on the right bank of the Clyde. Soon the immense timber-yards were thronged with spectators; not a part of the quay, not a wall of the wharf, not a factory roof showed an unoccupied place; the river itself was covered with craft of all descriptions, and the heights of Govan, on the left bank, swarmed with spectators.

There was, however, nothing extraordinary in the event about to take place; it was nothing but the launching of a ship, and this was an everyday affair with the people of Glasgow. Had the Dolphin, then—for that was the name of the ship built by Messrs. Tod & MacGregor—some special peculiarity? To tell the truth, it had none.

It was a large ship, about 1,500 tons, in which everything combined to obtain superior speed. Her engines, of 500 horse-power, were from the workshops of Lancefield Forge; they worked two screws, one on either side the stern-post, completely independent of each other. As for the depth of water the Dolphin would draw, it must be very inconsiderable; connoisseurs were not deceived, and they concluded rightly that this ship was destined for shallow straits. But all these particulars could not in any way justify the eagerness of the people: taken altogether, the Dolphin was nothing more or less than an ordinary ship. Would her launching present some mechanical difficulty to be overcome? Not any more than usual. The Clyde had received many a ship of heavier tonnage, and the launching of the Dolphin would take place in the usual manner.

In fact, when the water was calm, the moment the ebb-tide set in, the workmen began to operate. Their mallets kept perfect time falling on the wedges meant to raise the ship's keel: soon a shudder ran through the whole of her massive structure; although she had only been slightly raised, one could see that she shook, and then gradually began to glide down the well greased wedges, and in a few moments she plunged into the Clyde. Her stern struck the muddy bed of the river, then she raised herself on the top of a gigantic wave, and, carried forward by her start, would have been dashed against the quay of the Govan timber-yards, if her anchors had not restrained her.

The launch had been perfectly successful, the Dolphin swayed quietly on the waters of the Clyde, all the spectators clapped their hands when she took possession of her natural element, and loud hurrahs arose from either bank.

But wherefore these cries and this applause? Undoubtedly the most eager of the spectators would have been at a loss to explain the reason of his enthusiasm. What was the cause, then, of the lively interest excited by this ship? Simply the mystery which shrouded her destination; it was not known to what kind of commerce she was to be appropriated, and in questioning different groups the diversity of opinion on this important subject was indeed astonishing.

However, the best informed, at least those who pretended to be so, agreed in saying that the steamer was going to take part in the terrible war which was then ravaging the United States of America, but more than this they did not know, and whether the Dolphin was a privateer, a transport ship, or an addition to the Federal marine was what no one could tell.

"Hurrah!" cried one, affirming that the Dolphin had been built for the Southern States.

"Hip! hip! hip!" cried another, swearing that never had a faster boat crossed to the American coasts.

Thus its destination was unknown, and in order to obtain any reliable information one must be an intimate friend, or, at any rate, an acquaintance of Vincent Playfair & Co., of Glasgow.

A rich, powerful, intelligent house of business was that of Vincent Playfair & Co., in a social sense, an old and honourable family, descended from those tobacco lords who built the finest quarters of the town. These clever merchants, by an act of the Union, had founded the first Glasgow warehouse for dealing in tobacco from Virginia and Maryland. Immense fortunes were realised; mills and foundries sprang up in all parts, and in a few years the prosperity of the city attained its height.

The house of Playfair remained faithful to the enterprising spirit of its ancestors, it entered into the most daring schemes, and maintained the honour of English commerce. The principal, Vincent Playfair, a man of fifty, with a temperament essentially practical and decided, although somewhat daring, was a genuine shipowner. Nothing affected him beyond commercial questions, not even the political side of the transactions, otherwise he was a perfectly loyal and honest man.

However, he could not lay claim to the idea of building and fitting up the Dolphin; she belonged to his nephew, James Playfair, a fine young man of thirty, the boldest skipper of the British merchant marine.

It was one day at the Tontine coffee-room under the arcades of the town hall, that James Playfair, after having impatiently scanned the American journal, disclosed to his uncle an adventurous scheme.

"Uncle Vincent," said he, coming to the point at once, "there are two millions of pounds to be gained in less than a month."

"And what to risk?" asked Uncle Vincent.

"A ship and a cargo."

"Nothing else?"

"Nothing, except the crew and the captain, and that does not reckon for much."

"Let us see," said Uncle Vincent.

"It is all seen," replied James Playfair. "You have read the Tribune, the New York Herald, The Times, the Richmond Inquirer, the American Review?"

"Scores of times, nephew."

"You believe, like me, that the war of the United States will last a long time still?"

"A very long time."

"You know how much this struggle will affect the interests of England, and especially those of Glasgow?"

"And more especially still the house of Playfair & Co.," replied Uncle Vincent.

"Theirs especially," added the young Captain.

"I worry myself about it every day, James, and I cannot think without terror of the commercial disasters which this war may produce; not but that the house of Playfair is firmly established, nephew; at the same time it has correspondents which may fail. Ah! those Americans, slave-holders or Abolitionists, I have no faith in them!"

If Vincent Playfair was wrong in thus speaking with respect to the great principles of humanity, always and everywhere superior to personal interests, he was, nevertheless, right from a commercial point of view. The most important material was failing at Glasgow, the cotton famine became every day more threatening, thousands of workmen were reduced to living upon public charity. Glasgow possessed 25,000 looms, by which 625,000 yards of cotton were spun daily; that is to say, fifty millions of pounds yearly. From these numbers it may be guessed what disturbances were caused in the commercial part of the town when the raw material failed altogether. Failures were hourly taking place, the manufactories were closed, and the workmen were dying of starvation.

It was the sight of this great misery which had put the idea of his bold enterprise into James Playfair's head.

"I will go for cotton, and will get it, cost what it may."

But, as he also was a merchant as well as his uncle Vincent, he resolved to carry out his plan by way of exchange, and to make his proposition under the guise of a commercial enterprise.

"Uncle Vincent," said he, "this is my idea."

"Well, James?"

"It is simply this: we will have a ship built of superior sailing qualities and great bulk."

"That is quite possible."

"We will load her with ammunition of war, provisions, and clothes."

"Just so."

"I will take the command of this steamer, I will defy all the ships of the Federal marine for speed, and I will run the blockade of one of the southern ports."

"You must make a good bargain for your cargo with the Confederates, who will be in need of it," said his uncle.

"And I shall return laden with cotton."

"Which they will give you for nothing."

"As you say, Uncle. Will it answer?"

"It will; but shall you be able to get there?"

"I shall, if I have a good ship."

"One can be made on purpose. But the crew?"

"Oh, I will find them. I do not want many men; enough to work with, that is all. It is not a question of fighting with the Federals, but distancing them."

"They shall be distanced," said Uncle Vincent, in a peremptory tone; "but now, tell me, James, to what port of the American coast do you think of going?"

"Up to now, Uncle, ships have run the blockade of New Orleans, Wilmington, and Savannah, but I think of going straight to Charleston; no English boat has yet been able to penetrate into the harbour, except the Bermuda. I will do like her, and, if my ship draws but very little water, I shall be able to go where the Federalists will not be able to follow."

"The fact is," said Uncle Vincent, "Charleston is overwhelmed with cotton; they are even burning it to get rid of it."

"Yes," replied James; "besides, the town is almost invested; Beauregard is running short of provisions, and he will pay me a golden price for my cargo!"

"Well, nephew, and when will you start?"

"In six months; I must have the long winter nights to aid me."

"It shall be as you wish, nephew."

"It is settled, then, Uncle?"

"Settled!"

"Shall it be kept quiet?"

"Yes; better so."

And this is how it was that five months later the steamer Dolphin was launched from the Kelvin Dock timber-yards, and no one knew her real destination.

GETTING UNDER SAIL

The Dolphin was rapidly equipped, her rigging was ready, and there was nothing to do but fit her up. She carried three schooner-masts, an almost useless luxury; in fact, the Dolphin did not rely on the wind to escape the Federalists, but rather on her powerful engines.

Towards the end of December a trial of the steamer was made in the gulf of the Clyde. Which was the more satisfied, builder or captain, it is impossible to say. The new steamer shot along wonderfully, and the patent log showed a speed of seventeen miles an hour, a speed which as yet no English, French, or American boat had ever obtained. The Dolphin would certainly have gained by several lengths in a sailing match with the fastest opponent.

The loading was begun on the 25th of December, the steamer having ranged along the steamboat-quay a little below Glasgow Bridge, the last which stretches across the Clyde before its mouth. Here the wharfs were heaped with a heavy cargo of clothes, ammunition, and provisions which were rapidly carried to the hold of the Dolphin. The nature of this cargo betrayed the mysterious destination of the ship, and the house of Playfair could no longer keep it secret; besides, the Dolphin must not be long before she started. No American cruiser had been signalled in English waters; and, then, when the question of getting the crew came, how was it possible to keep silent any longer? They could not embark them, even, without informing the men whither they were bound, for, after all, it was a matter of life and death, and when one risks one's life, at least it is satisfactory to know how and wherefore.

However, this prospect hindered no one; the pay was good, and everyone had a share in the speculation, so that a great number of the finest sailors soon presented themselves. James Playfair was only embarrassed which to choose, but he chose well, and in twenty-four hours his muster-roll bore the names of thirty sailors who would have done honour to her Majesty's yacht.

The departure was settled for the 3rd of January; on the 31st of December the Dolphin was ready, her hold full of ammunition and provisions, and nothing was keeping her now.

The skipper went on board on the 2nd of January, and was giving a last look round his ship with a captain's eye, when a man presented himself at the fore part of the Dolphin, and asked to speak with the Captain. One of the sailors led him on to the poop.

He was a strong, hearty-looking fellow, with broad shoulders and ruddy face, the simple expression of which ill-concealed a depth of wit and mirth.

He did not seem to be accustomed to a seafaring life, and looked about him with the air of a man little used to being on board a ship; however, he assumed the manner of a Jack-tar, looking up at the rigging of the Dolphin, and waddling in true sailor fashion.

When he had reached the Captain, he looked fixedly at him, and said, "Captain James Playfair?"

"The same," replied the skipper. "What do you want with me?"

"To join your ship."

"There is no room; the crew is already complete."

"Oh, one man, more or less, will not be in the way; quite the contrary."

"You think so?" said James Playfair, giving a sidelong glance at his questioner.

"I am sure of it," replied the sailor.

"But who are you?" asked the Captain.

"A rough sailor, with two strong arms, which, I can tell you, are not to be despised on board a ship, and which I now have the honour of putting at your service."

"But there are other ships besides the Dolphin, and other captains besides James Playfair. Why do you come here?"

"Because it is on board the Dolphin that I wish to serve, and under the orders of Captain James Playfair."

"I do not want you."

"There is always need of a strong man, and if to prove my strength you will try me with three or four of the strongest fellows of your crew, I am ready."

"That will do," replied James Playfair. "And what is your name?"

"Crockston, at your service."

The Captain made a few steps backwards in order to get a better view of the giant who presented himself in this odd fashion. The height, the build, and the look of the sailor did not deny his pretensions to strength.

"Where have you sailed?" asked Playfair of him.

"A little everywhere."

"And do you know where the Dolphin is bound for?"

"Yes; and that is what tempts me."

"Ah, well! I have no mind to let a fellow of your stamp escape me. Go and find the first mate, and get him to enrol you."

Having said this, the Captain expected to see the man turn on his heels and run to the bows, but he was mistaken. Crockston did not stir.

"Well! did you hear me?" asked the Captain.

"Yes, but it is not all," replied the sailor. "I have something else to ask you."

"Ah! You are wasting my time," replied James, sharply; "I have not a moment to lose in talking."

"I shall not keep you long," replied Crockston; "two words more and that is all; I was going to tell you that I have a nephew."

"He has a fine uncle, then," interrupted James Playfair.

"Hah! Hah!" laughed Crockston.

"Have you finished?" asked the Captain, very impatiently.

"Well, this is what I have to say, when one takes the uncle, the nephew comes into the bargain."

"Ah! indeed!"

"Yes, that is the custom, the one does not go without the other."

"And what is this nephew of yours?"

"A lad of fifteen whom I am going to train to the sea; he is willing to learn, and will make a fine sailor some day."

"How now, Master Crockston," cried James Playfair; "do you think the Dolphin is a training-school for cabin-boys?"

"Don't let us speak ill of cabin-boys: there was one of them who became Admiral Nelson, and another Admiral Franklin."

"Upon my honour, friend," replied James Playfair, "you have a way of speaking which I like; bring your nephew, but if I don't find the uncle the hearty fellow he pretends to be, he will have some business with me. Go, and be back in an hour."

Crockston did not want to be told twice; he bowed awkwardly to the Captain of the Dolphin, and went on to the quay. An hour afterwards he came on board with his nephew, a boy of fourteen or fifteen, rather delicate and weakly looking, with a timid and astonished air, which showed that he did not possess his uncle's self-possession and vigorous corporeal qualities. Crockston was even obliged to encourage him by such words as these:

"Come," said he, "don't be frightened, they are not going to eat us, besides, there is yet time to return."

"No, no," replied the young man, "and may God protect us!"

The same day the sailor Crockston and his nephew were inscribed in the muster-roll of the Dolphin.

The next morning, at five o'clock, the fires of the steamer were well fed, the deck trembled under the vibrations of the boiler, and the steam rushed hissing through the escape-pipes. The hour of departure had arrived.

A considerable crowd, in spite of the early hour, flocked on the quays and on Glasgow Bridge; they had come to salute the bold steamer for the last time. Vincent Playfair was there to say good-bye to Captain James, but he conducted himself on this occasion like a Roman of the good old times. His was a heroic countenance, and the two loud kisses with which he gratified his nephew were the indication of a strong mind.

"Go, James," said he to the young Captain, "go quickly, and come back quicker still; above all, don't abuse your position. Sell at a good price, make a good bargain, and you will have your uncle's esteem."

On this recommendation, borrowed from the manual of the perfect merchant, the uncle and nephew separated, and all the visitors left the boat.

At this moment Crockston and John Stiggs stood together on the forecastle, while the former remarked to his nephew, "This is well, this is well; before two o'clock we shall be at sea, and I have a good opinion of a voyage which begins like this."

For reply the novice pressed Crockston's hand.

James Playfair then gave the orders for departure.

"Have we pressure on?" he asked of his mate.

"Yes, Captain," replied Mr. Mathew.

"Well, then, weigh anchor."

This was immediately done, and the screws began to move. The Dolphin trembled, passed between the ships in the port, and soon disappeared from the sight of the people, who shouted their last hurrahs.

The descent of the Clyde was easily accomplished, one might almost say that this river had been made by the hand of man, and even by the hand of a master. For sixty years, thanks to the dredges and constant dragging, it has gained fifteen feet in depth, and its breadth has been tripled between the quays and the town. Soon the forests of masts and chimneys were lost in the smoke and fog; the noise of the foundry hammers and the hatchets of the timber-yards grew fainter in the distance. After the village of Partick had been passed the factories gave way to country houses and villas. The Dolphin, slackening her speed, sailed between the dykes which carry the river above the shores, and often through a very narrow channel, which, however, is only a small inconvenience for a navigable river, for, after all, depth is of more importance than width. The steamer, guided by one of those excellent pilots from the Irish sea, passed without hesitation between floating buoys, stone columns, and biggings, surmounted with lighthouses, which mark the entrance to the channel. Beyond the town of Renfrew, at the foot of Kilpatrick hills, the Clyde grew wider. Then came Bouling Bay, at the end of which opens the mouth of the canal which joints Edinburgh to Glasgow. Lastly, at the height of four hundred feet from the ground, was seen the outline of Dumbarton Castle, almost indiscernible through the mists, and soon the harbour-boats of Glasgow were rocked on the waves which the Dolphin caused. Some miles farther on Greenock, the birthplace of James Watt, was passed: the Dolphin now found herself at the mouth of the Clyde, and at the entrance of the gulf by which it empties its waters into the Northern Ocean. Here the first undulations of the sea were felt, and the steamer ranged along the picturesque coast of the Isle of Arran. At last the promontory of Cantyre, which runs out into the channel, was doubled; the Isle of Rattelin was hailed, the pilot returned by a shore-boat to his cutter, which was cruising in the open sea; the Dolphin, returning to her Captain's authority, took a less frequented route round the north of Ireland, and soon, having lost sight of the last European land, found herself in the open ocean.

THINGS ARE NOT WHAT THEY SEEM

The Dolphin had a good crew, not fighting men, or boarding sailors, but good working men, and that was all she wanted. These brave, determined fellows were all, more or less, merchants; they sought a fortune rather than glory; they had no flag to display, no colours to defend with cannon; in fact, all the artillery on board consisted of two small swivel signal-guns.

The Dolphin shot bravely across the water, and fulfilled the utmost expectations of both builder and captain. Soon she passed the limit of British seas; there was not a ship in sight; the great ocean route was free; besides, no ship of the Federal marine would have a right to attack her beneath the English flag. Followed she might be, and prevented from forcing the blockade, and precisely for this reason had James Playfair sacrificed everything to the speed of his ship, in order not to be pursued.

Howbeit a careful watch was kept on board, and, in spite of the extreme cold, a man was always in the rigging ready to signal the smallest sail that appeared on the horizon. When evening came, Captain James gave the most precise orders to Mr. Mathew.

"Don't leave the man on watch too long in the rigging; the cold may seize him, and in that case it is impossible to keep a good look-out; change your men often."

"I understand, Captain," replied Mr. Mathew.

"Try Crockston for that work; the fellow pretends to have excellent sight; it must be put to trial; put him on the morning watch, he will have the morning mists to see through. If anything particular happens call me."

This said, James Playfair went to his cabin. Mr. Mathew called Crockston, and told him the Captain's orders.

"To-morrow, at six o'clock," said he, "you are to relieve watch of the main masthead."

For reply, Crockston gave a decided grunt, but Mr. Mathew had hardly turned his back when the sailor muttered some incomprehensible words, and then cried:

"What on earth did he say about the mainmast?"

At this moment his nephew, John Stiggs, joined him on the forecastle.

"Well, my good Crockston," said he.

"It's all right, all right," said the seaman, with a forced smile; "there is only one thing, this wretched boat shakes herself like a dog coming out of the water, and it makes my head confused."

"Dear Crockston, and it is for my sake."

"For you and him," replied Crockston, "but not a word about that, John. Trust in God, and He will not forsake you."

So saying, John Stiggs and Crockston went to the sailor's berth, but the sailor did not lie down before he had seen the young novice comfortably settled in the narrow cabin which he had got for him.

The next day, at six o'clock in the morning, Crockston got up to go to his place; he went on deck, where the first officer ordered him to go up into the rigging, and keep good watch.

At these words the sailor seemed undecided what to do; then, making up his mind, he went towards the bows of the Dolphin.

"Well, where are you off to now?" cried Mr. Mathew.

"Where you sent me," answered Crockston.

"I told you to go to the mainmast."

"And I am going there," replied the sailor, in an unconcerned tone, continuing his way to the poop.

"Are you a fool?" cried Mr. Mathew, impatiently; "you are looking for the bars of the main on the foremast. You are like a cockney, who doesn't know how to twist a cat-o'-nine-tails, or make a splice. On board what ship can you have been, man? The mainmast, stupid, the mainmast!"

The sailors who had run up to hear what was going on burst out laughing when they saw Crockston's disconcerted look, as he went back to the forecastle.

"So," said he, looking up the mast, the top of which was quite invisible through the morning mists; "so, am I to climb up here?"

"Yes," replied Mr. Mathew, "and hurry yourself! By St. Patrick, a Federal ship would have time to get her bowsprit fast in our rigging before that lazy fellow could get to his post. Will you go up?"

Without a word, Crockston got on the bulwarks with some difficulty; then he began to climb the rigging with most visible awkwardness, like a man who did not know how to make use of his hands or feet. When he had reached the topgallant, instead of springing lightly on to it, he remained motionless, clinging to the ropes, as if he had been seized with giddiness. Mr. Mathew, irritated by his stupidity, ordered him to come down immediately.

"That fellow there," said he to the boatswain, "has never been a sailor in his life. Johnston, just go and see what he has in his bundle."

The boatswain made haste to the sailor's berth.

In the meantime Crockston was with difficulty coming down again, but, his foot having slipped, he slid down the rope he had hold of, and fell heavily on the deck.

"Clumsy blockhead! land-lubber!" cried Mr. Mathew, by way of consolation. "What did you come to do on board the Dolphin! Ah! you entered as an able seaman, and you cannot even distinguish the main from the foremast! I shall have a little talk with you."

Crockston made no attempt to speak; he bent his back like a man resigned to anything he might have to bear; just then the boatswain returned.

"This," said he to the first officer, "is all that I have found; a suspicious portfolio with letters."

"Give them here," said Mr. Mathew. "Letters with Federal stamps! Mr. Halliburtt, of Boston! An Abolitionist! a Federalist! Wretch! you are nothing but a traitor, and have sneaked on board to betray us! Never mind, you will be paid for your trouble with the cat-o'-nine-tails! Boatswain, call the Captain, and you others just keep an eye on that rogue there."

Crockston received these compliments with a hideous grimace, but he did not open his lips. They had fastened him to the capstan, and he could move neither hand nor foot.

A few minutes later James Playfair came out of his cabin and went to the forecastle, where Mr. Mathew immediately acquainted him with the details of the case.

"What have you to say?" asked James Playfair, scarcely able to restrain his anger.

"Nothing," replied Crockston.

"And what did you come on board my ship for?"

"Nothing."

"And what do you expect from me now?"

"Nothing."

"Who are you? An American, as letters seem to prove?" Crockston did not answer.

"Boatswain," said James Playfair, "fifty lashes with the cat-o'-nine-tails to loosen his tongue. Will that be enough, Crockston?"

"It will remain to be seen," replied John Stiggs' uncle without moving a muscle.

"Now then, come along, men," said the boatswain.

At this order, two strong sailors stripped Crockston of his woollen jersey; they had already seized the formidable weapon, and laid it across the prisoner's shoulders, when the novice, John Stiggs, pale and agitated, hurried on deck.

"Captain!" exclaimed he.

"Ah! the nephew!" remarked James Playfair.

"Captain," repeated the novice, with a violent effort to steady his voice, "I will tell you what Crockston does not want to say. I will hide it no longer; yes, he is American, and so am I; we are both enemies of the slave-holders, but not traitors come on board to betray the Dolphin into the hands of the Federalists."

"What did you come to do, then?" asked the Captain, in a severe tone, examining the novice attentively. The latter hesitated a few seconds before replying, then he said, "Captain, I should like to speak to you in private."

Whilst John Stiggs made this request, James Playfair did not cease to look carefully at him; the sweet young face of the novice, his peculiarly gentle voice, the delicacy and whiteness of his hands, hardly disguised by paint, the large eyes, the animation of which could not bide their tenderness—all this together gave rise to a certain suspicion in the Captain's mind. When John Stiggs had made his request, Playfair glanced fixedly at Crockston, who shrugged his shoulders; then he fastened a questioning look on the novice, which the latter could not withstand, and said simply to him, "Come."

John Stiggs followed the Captain on to the poop, and then James Playfair, opening the door of his cabin, said to the novice, whose cheeks were pale with emotion, "Be so kind as to walk in, miss."

John, thus addressed, blushed violently, and two tears rolled involuntarily down his cheeks.

"Don't be alarmed, miss," said James Playfair, in a gentle voice, "but be so good as to tell me how I come to have the honour of having you on board?"

The young girl hesitated a moment, then, reassured by the Captain's look, she made up her mind to speak.

"Sir," said she, "I wanted to join my father at Charleston; the town is besieged by land and blockaded by sea. I knew not how to get there, when I heard that the Dolphin meant to force the blockade. I came on board your ship, and I beg you to forgive me if I acted without your consent, which you would have refused me."

"Certainly," said James Playfair.

"I did well, then, not to ask you," resumed the young girl, with a firmer voice.

The Captain crossed his arms, walked round his cabin, and then came back.

"What is your name?" said he.

"Jenny Halliburtt."

"Your father, if I remember rightly the address on the letters, is he not from Boston?"

"Yes, sir."

"And a Northerner is thus in a southern town in the thickest of the war?"

"My father is a prisoner; he was at Charleston when the first shot of the Civil War was fired, and the troops of the Union driven from Fort Sumter by the Confederates. My father's opinions exposed him to the hatred of the slavist part, and by the order of General Beauregard he was imprisoned. I was then in England, living with a relation who has just died, and left alone, with no help but that of Crockston, our faithful servant, I wished to go to my father and share his prison with him."

"What was Mr. Halliburtt, then?" asked James Playfair.

"A loyal and brave journalist," replied Jenny proudly, "one of the noblest editors of the Tribune, and the one who was the boldest in defending the cause of the negroes."

"An Abolitionist," cried the Captain angrily; "one of those men who, under the vain pretence of abolishing slavery, have deluged their country with blood and ruin."

"Sir!" replied Jenny Halliburtt, growing pale, "you are insulting my father; you must not forget that I stand alone to defend him."

The young Captain blushed scarlet; anger mingled with shame struggled in his breast; perhaps he would have answered the young girl, but he succeeded in restraining himself, and, opening the door of the cabin, he called "Boatswain!"

The boatswain came to him directly.

"This cabin will henceforward belong to Miss Jenny Halliburtt. Have a cot made ready for me at the end of the poop; that's all I want."

The boatswain looked with a stupefied stare at the young novice addressed in a feminine name, but on a sign from James Playfair he went out.

"And now, miss, you are at home," said the young Captain of the Dolphin. Then he retired.

CROCKSTON⬜S TRICK

It was not long before the whole crew knew Miss Halliburtt's story, which Crockston was no longer hindered from telling. By the Captain's orders he was released from the capstan, and the cat-o'-nine-tails returned to its Place.

"A pretty animal," said Crockston, "especially when it shows its velvety paws."

As soon as he was free, he went down to the sailors' berths, found a small portmanteau, and carried it to Miss Jenny; the young girl was now able to resume her feminine attire, but she remained in her cabin, and did not again appear on deck.

As for Crockston, it was well and duly agreed that, as he was no more a sailor than a horse-guard, he should be exempt from all duty on board.

In the meanwhile the Dolphin, with her twin screws cutting the waves, sped rapidly across the Atlantic, and there was nothing now to do but keep a strict look-out. The day following the discovery of Miss Jenny's identity, James Playfair paced the deck at the poop with a rapid step; he had made no attempt to see the young girl and resume the conversation of the day before.

Whilst he was walking to and fro, Crockston passed him several times, looking at him askant with a satisfied grin. He evidently wanted to speak to the Captain, and at last his persistent manner attracted the attention of the latter, who said to him, somewhat impatiently:

"How now, what do you want? You are turning round me like a swimmer round a buoy: when are you going to leave off?"

"Excuse me, Captain," answered Crockston, winking, "I wanted to speak to you."

"Speak, then."

"Oh, it is nothing very much. I only wanted to tell you frankly that you are a good fellow at bottom."

"Why at bottom?"

"At bottom and surface also."

"I don't want your compliments."

"I am not complimenting you. I shall wait to do that when you have gone to the end."

"To what end?"

"To the end of your task."

"Ah! I have a task to fulfil?"

"Decidedly, you have taken the young girl and myself on board; good! You have given up your cabin to Miss Halliburtt; good! You released me from the cat-o'-nine-tails; nothing could be better. You are going to take us straight to Charleston; that's delightful, but it is not all."

"How not all?" cried James Playfair, amazed at Crockston's boldness.

"No, certainly not," replied the latter, with a knowing look, "the father is prisoner there."

"Well, what about that?"

"Well, the father must be rescued."

"Rescue Miss Halliburtt's father?"

"Most certainly, and it is worth risking something for such a noble man and courageous citizen as he."

"Master Crockston," said James Playfair, frowning, "I am not in the humour for your jokes, so have a care what you say."

"You misunderstand me, Captain," said the American. "I am not joking in the least, but speaking quite seriously. What I have proposed may at first seem very absurd to you; when you have thought it over, you will see that you cannot do otherwise."

"What, do you mean that I must deliver Mr. Halliburtt?"

"Just so. You can demand his release of General Beauregard, who will not refuse you."

"But if he does refuse me?"

"In that case," replied Crockston, in a deliberate tone, "we must use stronger measures, and carry off the prisoner by force."

"So," cried James Playfair, who was beginning to get angry, "so, not content with passing through the Federal fleets and forcing the blockade of Charleston, I must run out to sea again from under the cannon of the forts, and this to deliver a gentleman I know nothing of, one of those Abolitionists whom I detest, one of those journalists who shed ink instead of their blood!"

"Oh, it is but a cannon-shot more or less!" added Crockston.

"Master Crockston," said James Playfair, "mind what I say: if ever you mention this affair again to me, I will send you to the hold for the rest of the passage, to teach you manners."

Thus saying, the Captain dismissed the American, who went off murmuring, "Ah, well, I am not altogether displeased with this conversation: at any rate, the affair is broached; it will do, it will do!"

James Playfair had hardly meant it when he said an Abolitionist whom I detest; he did not in the least side with the Federals, but he did not wish to admit that the question of slavery was the predominant reason for the civil war of the United States, in spite of President Lincoln's formal declaration. Did he, then, think that the Southern States, eight out of thirty-six, were right in separating when they had been voluntarily united?

Not so; he detested the Northerners, and that was all; he detested them as brothers separated from the common family—true Englishmen—who had thought it right to do what he, James Playfair, disapproved of with regard to the United States: these were the political opinions of the Captain of the Dolphin. But, more than this, the American war interfered with him personally, and he had a grudge against those who had caused this war; one can understand, then, how he would receive a proposition to deliver an Abolitionist, thus bringing down on him the Confederates, with whom he pretended to do business.

However, Crockston's insinuation did not fail to disturb him; he cast the thought from him, but it returned unceasingly to his mind, and when Miss Jenny came on deck the next day for a few minutes, he dared not look her in the face.

And really it was a great pity, for this young girl, with the fair hair and sweet, intelligent face, deserved to be looked at by a young man of thirty. But James felt embarrassed in her presence; he felt that this charming creature who had been educated in the school of misfortune possessed a strong and generous soul; he understood that his silence towards her inferred a refusal to acquiesce in her dearest wishes; besides, Miss Jenny never looked out for James Playfair, neither did she avoid him. Thus for the first few days they spoke little or not at all to each other. Miss Halliburtt scarcely ever left her cabin, and it is certain she would never have addressed herself to the Captain of the Dolphin if it had not been for Crockston's strategy, which brought both parties together.

The worthy American was a faithful servant of the Halliburtt family; he had been brought up in his master's house, and his devotion knew no bounds. His good sense equalled his courage and energy, and, as has been seen, he had a way of looking things straight in the face. He was very seldom discouraged, and could generally find a way out of the most intricate dangers with a wonderful skill.

This honest fellow had taken it into his head to deliver Mr. Halliburtt, to employ the Captain's ship, and the Captain himself for this purpose, and to return with him to England. Such was his intention, so long as the young girl had no other object than to rejoin her father and share his captivity. It was this Crockston tried to make the Captain understand, as we have seen, but the enemy had not yet surrendered; on the contrary.

"Now," said he, "it is absolutely necessary that Miss Jenny and the Captain come to an understanding; if they are going to be sulky like this all the passage we shall get nothing done. They must speak, discuss; let them dispute even, so long as they talk, and I'll be hanged if during their conversation James Playfair does not propose himself what he refused me to-day."

But when Crockston saw that the young girl and the young man avoided each other, he began to be perplexed.

"We must look sharp," said he to himself, and the morning of the fourth day he entered Miss Halliburtt's cabin, rubbing his hands with an air of perfect satisfaction.

"Good news!" cried he, "good news! You will never guess what the Captain has proposed to me. A very noble young man he is. Now try."

"Ah!" replied Jenny, whose heart beat violently, "has he proposed to—"

"To deliver Mr. Halliburtt, to carry him off from the Confederates, and bring him to England."

"Is it true?" cried Jenny.

"It is as I say, miss. What a good-hearted man this James Playfair is! These English are either all good or all bad. Ah! he may reckon on my gratitude, and I am ready to cut myself in pieces if it would please him."

Jenny's joy was profound on hearing Crockston's words. Deliver her father! She had never dared to think of such a plan, and the Captain of the Dolphin was going to risk his ship and crew!

"That's what he is," added Crockston; "and this, Miss Jenny, is well worth an acknowledgment from you."

"More than an acknowledgment," cried the young girl; "a lasting friendship!"

And immediately she left the cabin to find James Playfair, and express to him the sentiments which flowed from her heart.

"Getting on by degrees," muttered the American.

James Playfair was pacing to and fro on the poop, and, as may be thought, he was very much surprised, not to say amazed, to see the young girl come up to him, her eyes moist with grateful tears, and, holding out her hand to him, saying:

"Thank you, sir, thank you for your kindness, which I should never have dared to expect from a stranger."

"Miss," replied the Captain, as if he understood nothing of what she was talking, and could not understand, "I do not know—"

"Nevertheless, sir, you are going to brave many dangers, perhaps compromise your interests for me, and you have done so much already in offering me on board an hospitality to which I have no right whatever—"

"Pardon me, Miss Jenny," interrupted James Playfair, "but I protest again I do not understand your words. I have acted towards you as any well-bred man would towards a lady, and my conduct deserves neither so many thanks nor so much gratitude."

"Mr. Playfair," said Jenny, "it is useless to pretend any longer; Crockston has told me all!"

"Ah!" said the Captain, "Crockston has told you all; then I understand less than ever the reason for your leaving your cabin, and saying these words which—"

Whilst speaking the Captain felt very much embarrassed; he remembered the rough way in which he had received the American's overtures, but Jenny, fortunately for him, did not give him time for further explanation; she interrupted him, holding out her hand and saying:

"Mr. James, I had no other object in coming on board your ship except to go to Charleston, and there, however cruel the slave-holders may be, they will not refuse to let a poor girl share her father's prison; that was all. I had never thought of a return as possible; but, since you are so generous as to wish for my father's deliverance, since you will attempt everything to save him, be assured you have my deepest gratitude."

James did not know what to do or what part to assume; he bit his lip; he dared not take the hand offered him; he saw perfectly that Crockston had compromised him, so that escape was impossible. At the same time he had no thoughts of delivering Mr. Halliburtt, and getting complicated in a disagreeable business: but how dash to the ground the hope which had arisen in this poor girl's heart? How refuse the hand which she held out to him with a feeling of such profound friendship? How change to tears of grief the tears of gratitude which filled her eyes?

So the young man tried to reply evasively, in a manner which would ensure his liberty of action for the future.

"Miss Jenny," said he, "rest assured I will do everything in my power for—"

And he took the little hand in both of his, but with the gentle pressure he felt his heart melt and his head grow confused: words to express his thoughts failed him. He stammered out some incoherent words:

"Miss—Miss Jenny—for you—"

Crockston, who was watching him, rubbed his hands, grinning and repeating to himself:

"It will come! it will come! it has come!"

How James Playfair would have managed to extricate himself from his embarrassing position no one knows, but fortunately for him, if not for the Dolphin, the man on watch was heard crying:

"Ahoy, officer of the watch!"

"What now?" asked Mr. Mathew.

"A sail to windward!"

James Playfair, leaving the young girl, immediately sprang to the shrouds of the mainmast.

THE SHOT FROM THE IROQUOIS, AND MISS JENNY'S ARGUMENTS

Until now the navigation of the Dolphin had been very fortunate. Not one ship had been signalled before the sail hailed by the man on watch.

The Dolphin was then in 32° 51' lat., and 57° 43' W. longitude. For forty-eight hours a fog, which now began to rise, had covered the ocean. If this mist favoured the Dolphin by hiding her course, it also prevented any observations at a distance being made, and, without being aware of it, she might be sailing side by side, so to speak, with the ships she wished most to avoid.

Now this is just what had happened, and when the ship was signalled she was only three miles to windward.

When James Playfair had reached the cross-trees, he saw distinctly, through an opening in the mist, a large Federal corvette in full pursuit of the Dolphin.

After having carefully examined her, the Captain came down on deck again, and called to the first officer.

"Mr. Mathew," said he, "what do you think of this ship?"

"I think, Captain, that it is a Federal cruiser, which suspects our intentions."

"There is no possible doubt of her nationality," said James Playfair. "Look!"

At this moment the starry flag of the North United States appeared on the gaff-yards of the corvette, and the latter asserted her colours with a cannon-shot.

"An invitation to show ours," said Mr. Mathew. "Well, let us show them; there is nothing to be ashamed of."

"What's the good?" replied James Playfair. "Our flag will hardly protect us, and it will not hinder those people from paying us a visit. No; let us go ahead."

"And go quickly," replied Mr. Mathew, "for, if my eyes do not deceive me, I have already seen that corvette lying off Liverpool, where she went to watch the ships in building: my name is not Mathew, if that is not the Iroquois on her taffrail."

"And is she fast?"

"One of the fastest vessels of the Federal marine."

"What guns does she carry?"

"Eight."

"Pooh!"

"Oh, don't shrug your shoulders, Captain," said Mr. Mathew, in a serious tone; "two out of those eight guns are rifled, one is a sixty-pounder on the forecastle, and the other a hundred-pounder on deck."

"Upon my soul!" exclaimed James Playfair, "they are Parrott's, and will carry three miles."

"Yes, and farther than that, Captain."

"Ah, well! Mr. Mathew, let their guns be sixty or only four-pounders, and let them carry three miles or five hundred yards, it is all the same if we can go fast enough to avoid their shot. We will show this Iroquois how a ship can go when she is built on purpose to go. Have the fires drawn forward, Mr. Mathew."

The first officer gave the Captain's orders to the engineer, and soon volumes of black smoke curled from the steamer's chimneys.

This proceeding did not seem to please the corvette, for she made the Dolphin the signal to lie to, but James Playfair paid no attention to this warning, and did not change his ship's course.

"Now," said he, "we shall see what the Iroquois will do; here is a fine opportunity for her to try her guns. Go ahead full speed!"

"Good!" exclaimed Mr. Mathew; "she will not be long in saluting us."

Returning to the poop, the Captain saw Miss Halliburtt sitting quietly near the bulwarks.

"Miss Jenny," said he, "we shall probably be chased by that corvette you see to windward, and as she will speak to us with shot, I beg to offer you my arm to take you to your cabin again."

"Thank you, very much, Mr. Playfair," replied the young girl, looking at him, "but I am not afraid of cannon-shots."

"However, miss, in spite of the distance, there may be some danger."

"Oh, I was not brought up to be fearful; they accustom us to everything in America, and I assure you that the shot from the Iroquois will not make me lower my head."

"You are brave, Miss Jenny."

"Let us admit, then, that I am brave, and allow me to stay by you."

"I can refuse you nothing, Miss Halliburtt," replied the Captain, looking at the young girl's calm face.

These words were hardly uttered when they saw a line of white smoke issue from the bulwarks of the corvette; before the report had reached the Dolphin a projectile whizzed through the air in the direction of the steamer.

At about twenty fathoms from the Dolphin the shot, the speed of which had sensibly lessened, skimmed over the surface of the waves, marking its passage by a series of water-jets; then, with another burst, it rebounded to a certain height, passed over the Dolphin, grazing the mizzen-yards on the starboard side, fell at thirty fathoms beyond, and was buried in the waves.

"By Jove!" exclaimed James Playfair, "we must get along; another slap like that is not to be waited for."

"Oh!" exclaimed Mr. Mathew, "they will take some time to reload such pieces."

"Upon my honour, it is an interesting sight," said Crockston, who, with arms crossed, stood perfectly at his ease looking at the scene.

"Ah! that's you," cried James Playfair, scanning the American from head to foot.

"It is me, Captain," replied the American, undisturbed. "I have come to see how these brave Federals fire; not badly, in truth, not badly."

The Captain was going to answer Crockston sharply, but at this moment a second shot struck the sea on the starboard side.

"Good!" cried James Playfair, "we have already gained two cables on this Iroquois. Your friends sail like a buoy; do you hear, Master Crockston?"

"I will not say they don't," replied the American, "and for the first time in my life it does not fail to please me."

A third shot fell still farther astern, and in less than ten minutes the Dolphin was out of range of the corvette's guns.

"So much for patent-logs, Mr. Mathew," said James Playfair; "thanks to those shot we know how to rate our speed. Now have the fires lowered; it is not worth while to waste our coal uselessly."

"It is a good ship that you command," said Miss Halliburtt to the young Captain.

"Yes, Miss Jenny, my good Dolphin makes her seventeen knots, and before the day is over we shall have lost sight of that corvette."

James Playfair did not exaggerate the sailing qualities of his ship, and the sun had not set before the masts of the American ship had disappeared below the horizon.

This incident allowed the Captain to see Miss Halliburtt's character in a new light; besides, the ice was broken, henceforward, during the whole of the voyage; the interviews between the Captain and his passenger were frequent and prolonged; he found her to be a young girl, calm, strong, thoughtful, and intelligent, speaking with great ease, having her own ideas about everything, and expressing her thoughts with a conviction which unconsciously penetrated James Playfair's heart.

She loved her country, she was zealous in the great cause of the Union, and expressed herself on the civil war in the United States with an enthusiasm of which no other woman would have been capable. Thus it happened, more than once, that James Playfair found it difficult to answer her, even when questions purely mercantile arose in connection with the war: Miss Jenny attacked them none the less vigorously, and would come to no other terms whatever. At first James argued a great deal, and tried to uphold the Confederates against the Federals, to prove that the Secessionists were in the right, and that if the people were united voluntarily they might separate in the same manner. But the young girl would not yield on this point; she demonstrated that the question of slavery was predominant in the struggle between the North and South Americans, that it was far more a war in the cause of morals and humanity than politics, and James could make no answer. Besides, during these discussions, which he listened to attentively, it is difficult to say whether he was more touched by Miss Halliburtt's arguments or the charming manner in which she spoke; but at last he was obliged to acknowledge, among other things, that slavery was the principal feature in the war, that it must be put an end to decisively, and the last horrors of barbarous times abolished.

It has been said that the political opinions of the Captain did not trouble him much. He would have sacrificed his most serious opinion before such enticing arguments and under like circumstances; he made a good bargain of his ideas for the same reason, but at last he was attacked in his tenderest point; this was the question of the traffic in which the Dolphin was being employed, and, consequently, the ammunition which was being carried to the Confederates.

"Yes, Mr. James," said Miss Halliburtt, "gratitude does not hinder me from speaking with perfect frankness; on the contrary, you are a brave seaman, a clever merchant, the house of Playfair is noted for its respectability; but in this case it fails in its principles, and follows a trade unworthy of it."

"How!" cried James, "the house of Playfair ought not to attempt such a commercial enterprise?"

"No! it is taking ammunition to the unhappy creatures in revolt against the government of their country, and it is lending arms to a bad cause."

"Upon my honour, Miss Jenny, I will not discuss the right of the Confederates with you; I will only answer you with one word: I am a merchant, and as such I only occupy myself with the interests of my house; I look for gain wherever there is an opportunity of getting it."

"That is precisely what is to be blamed, Mr. James," replied the young girl; "profit does not excuse it; thus, when you supply arms to the Southerners, with which to continue a criminal war, you are quite as guilty as when you sell opium to the Chinese, which stupefies them."

"Oh, for once, Miss Jenny, this is too much, and I cannot admit—"

"No; what I say is just, and when you consider it, when you understand the part you are playing, when you think of the results for which you are responsible, you will yield to me in this point, as in so many others."

James Playfair was dumfounded at these words; he left the young girl, a prey to angry thoughts, for he felt his powerlessness to answer; then he sulked like a child for half an hour, and an hour later he returned to the singular young girl who could overwhelm him with convincing arguments with quite a pleasant smile.

In short, however it may have come about, and although he would not acknowledge it to himself, Captain James Playfair belonged to himself no longer; he was no longer commander-in-chief on board his own ship.

Thus, to Crockston's great joy, Mr. Halliburtt's affairs appeared to be in a good way; the Captain seemed to have decided to undertake everything in his power to deliver Miss Jenny's father, and for this he would be obliged to compromise the Dolphin, his cargo, his crew, and incur the displeasure of his worthy Uncle Vincent.

SULLIVAN ISLAND CHANNEL

Two days after the meeting with the Iroquois, the Dolphin found herself abreast of the Bermudas, where she was assailed by a violent squall. These isles are frequently visited by hurricanes, and are celebrated for shipwrecks. It is here that Shakespeare has placed the exciting scene of his drama, The Tempest, in which Ariel and Caliban dispute for the empire of the floods.

The squall was frightful; James Playfair thought once of running for one of the Bermudas, where the English had a military post: it would have been a sad waste of time, and therefore especially to be regretted; happily the Dolphin behaved herself wonderfully well in the storm, and, after flying a whole day before the tempest, she was able to resume her course towards the American coast.

But if James Playfair had been pleased with his ship, he had not been less delighted with the young girl's bravery; Miss Halliburtt had passed the worst hours of the storm at his side, and James knew that a profound, imperious, irresistible love had taken possession of his whole being.

"Yes," said he, "this brave girl is mistress on board; she turns me like the sea a ship in distress—I feel that I am foundering! What will Uncle Vincent say? Ah! poor nature, I am sure that if Jenny asked me to throw all this cursed cargo into the sea, I should do it without hesitating, for love of her."

Happily for the firm of Playfair & Co., Miss Halliburtt did not demand this sacrifice; nevertheless, the poor Captain had been taken captive, and Crockston, who read his heart like an open book, rubbed his hands gleefully.

"We will hold him fast!" he muttered to himself, "and before a week has passed my master will be quietly installed in one of the best cabins of the Dolphin."

As for Miss Jenny, did she perceive the feelings which she inspired? Did she allow herself to share them? No one could say, and James Playfair least of all; the young girl kept a perfect reserve, and her secret remained deeply buried in her heart.

But whilst love was making such progress in the heart of the young Captain, the Dolphin sped with no less rapidity towards Charleston.

On the 13th of January, the watch signalled land ten miles to the west. It was a low-lying coast, and almost blended with the line of the sea in the distance. Crockston was examining the horizon attentively, and about nine o'clock in the morning he cried:

"Charleston lighthouse!"

Now that the bearings of the Dolphin were set, James Playfair had but one thing to do, to decide by which channel he would run into Charleston Bay.

"If we meet with no obstacles," said he, "before three o'clock we shall be in safety in the docks of the port."

The town of Charleston is situated on the banks of an estuary seven miles long and two broad, called Charleston Harbour, the entrance to which is rather difficult. It is enclosed between Morris Island on the south and Sullivan Island on the north. At the time when the Dolphin attempted to force the blockade Morris Island already belonged to the Federal troops, and General Gillmore had caused batteries to be erected overlooking the harbour. Sullivan Island, on the contrary, was in the hands of the Confederates, who were also in possession of Moultrie Fort, situated at the extremity of the island; therefore it would be advantageous to the Dolphin to go as close as possible to the northern shores to avoid the firing from the forts on Morris Island.

Five channels led into the estuary, Sullivan Island Channel, the Northern Channel, the Overall Channel, the Principal Channel, and lastly, the Lawford Channel; but it was useless for strangers, unless they had skilful pilots on board, or ships drawing less than seven feet of water, to attempt this last; as for Northern and Overall Channels, they were in range of the Federalist batteries, so that it was no good thinking of them. If James Playfair could have had his choice, he would have taken his steamer through the Principal Channel, which was the best, and the bearings of which were easy to follow; but it was necessary to yield to circumstances, and to decide according to the event. Besides, the Captain of the Dolphin knew perfectly all the secrets of this bay, its dangers, the depths of its water at low tide, and its currents, so that he was able to steer his ship with the greatest safety as soon as he entered one of these narrow straits. The great question was to get there.

Now this work demanded an experienced seaman, and one who knew exactly the qualities of the Dolphin.

In fact, two Federal frigates were now cruising in the Charleston waters. Mr. Mathew soon drew James Playfair's attention to them.

"They are preparing to ask us what we want on these shores," said he.

"Ah, well! we won't answer them," replied the Captain, "and they will not get their curiosity satisfied."

In the meanwhile the cruisers were coming on full steam towards the Dolphin, who continued her course, taking care to keep out of range of their guns. But in order to gain time James Playfair made for the south-west, wishing to put the enemies' ships off their guard; the latter must have thought that the Dolphin intended to make for Morris Island Channel.

Now there they had batteries and guns, a single shot from which would have been enough to sink the English ship; so the Federals allowed the Dolphin to run towards the south-west, contenting themselves by observing her without following closely.

Thus for an hour the respective situations of the ships did not change, for James Playfair, wishing to deceive the cruisers as to the course of the Dolphin, had caused the fires to be moderated, so that the speed was decreased. However, from the thick volumes of smoke which escaped from the chimneys, it might have been thought that he was trying to get his maximum pressure, and, consequently his maximum of rapidity.

"They will be slightly astonished presently," said James Playfair, "when they see us slip through their fingers!"

In fact, when the Captain saw that he was near enough to Morris Island, and before a line of guns, the range of which he did not know, he turned his rudder quickly, and the ship resumed her northerly course, leaving the cruisers two miles to windward of her; the latter, seeing this manoeuvre, understood the steamer's object, and began to pursue her in earnest, but it was too late. The Dolphin doubled her speed under the action of the screws, and distanced them rapidly. Going nearer to the coast, a few shell were sent after her as an acquittal of conscience, but the Federals were outdone, for their projectiles did not reach half-way. At eleven o'clock in the morning, the steamer ranging near Sullivan Island, thanks to her small draft, entered the narrow strait full steam; there she was in safety, for no Federalist cruiser dared follow her in this channel, the depth of which, on an average, was only eleven feet at low tide.

"How!" cried Crockston, "and is that the only difficulty?"

"Oh! oh! Master Crockston," said James Playfair, "the difficulty is not in entering, but in getting out again."

"Nonsense!" replied the American, "that does not make me at all uneasy; with a boat like the Dolphin and a Captain like Mr. James Playfair, one can go where one likes, and come out in the same manner."

Nevertheless, James Playfair, with telescope in his hand, was attentively examining the route to be followed. He had before him excellent coasting guides, with which he could go ahead without any difficulty or hesitation.

Once his ship was safely in the narrow channel which runs the length of Sullivan Island, James steered bearing towards the middle of Fort Moultrie as far as the Pickney Castle, situated on the isolated island of Shute's Folly; on the other side rose Fort Johnson, a little way to the north of Fort Sumter.

At this moment the steamer was saluted by some shot which did not reach her, from the batteries on Morris Island. She continued her course without any deviation, passed before Moultrieville, situated at the extremity of Sullivan Island, and entered the bay.

Soon Fort Sumter on the left protected her from the batteries of the Federalists.

This fort, so celebrated in the civil war, is situated three miles and a half from Charleston, and about a mile from each side of the bay: it is nearly pentagonal in form, built on an artificial island of Massachusetts granite; it took ten years to construct and cost more than 900,000 dollars.

It was from this fort, on the 13th of April, 1861, that Anderson and the Federal troops were driven, and it was against it that the first shot of the Confederates was fired. It is impossible to estimate the quantity of iron and lead which the Federals showered down upon it. However, it resisted for almost three years, but a few months after the passage of the Dolphin it fell beneath General Gillmore's three hundred-pounders on Morris Island.

But at this time it was in all its strength, and the Confederate flag floated proudly above it.

Once past the fort, the town of Charleston appeared, lying between Ashley and Cooper Rivers.

James Playfair threaded his way through the buoys which mark the entrance of the channel, leaving behind the Charleston lighthouse, visible above Morris Island. He had hoisted the English flag, and made his way with wonderful rapidity through the narrow channels. When he had passed the quarantine buoy, he advanced freely into the centre of the bay. Miss Halliburtt was standing on the poop, looking at the town where her father was kept prisoner, and her eyes filled with tears.

At last the steamer's speed was moderated by the Captain's orders; the Dolphin ranged along the end of the south and east batteries, and was soon moored at the quay of the North Commercial Wharf.

A SOUTHERN GENERAL

The Dolphin, on arriving at the Charleston quay, had been saluted by the cheers of a large crowd. The inhabitants of this town, strictly blockaded by sea, were not accustomed to visits from European ships. They asked each other, not without astonishment, what this great steamer, proudly bearing the English flag, had come to do in their waters; but when they learned the object of her voyage, and why she had just forced the passage Sullivan, when the report spread that she carried a cargo of smuggled ammunition, the cheers and joyful cries were redoubled.

James Playfair, without losing a moment, entered into negotiation with General Beauregard, the military commander of the town. The latter eagerly received the young Captain of the Dolphin, who had arrived in time to provide the soldiers with the clothes and ammunition they were so much in want of. It was agreed that the unloading of the ship should take place immediately, and numerous hands came to help the English sailors.

Before quitting his ship James Playfair had received from Miss Halliburtt the most pressing injunctions with regard to her father, and the Captain had placed himself entirely at the young girl's service.

"Miss Jenny," he had said, "you may rely on me; I will do the utmost in my power to save your father, but I hope this business will not present many difficulties. I shall go and see General Beauregard to-day, and, without asking him at once for Mr. Halliburtt's liberty, I shall learn in what situation he is, whether he is on bail or a prisoner."

"My poor father!" replied Jenny, sighing; "he little thinks his daughter is so near him. Oh that I could fly into his arms!"

"A little patience, Miss Jenny; you will soon embrace your father. Rely upon my acting with the most entire devotion, but also with prudence and consideration."

This is why James Playfair, after having delivered the cargo of the Dolphin up to the General, and bargained for an immense stock of cotton, faithful to his promise, turned the conversation to the events of the day.

"So," said he, "you believe in the triumph of the slave-holders?"

"I do not for a moment doubt of our final success, and, as regards Charleston, Lee's army will soon relieve it: besides, what do you expect from the Abolitionists? Admitting that which will never be, that the commercial towns of Virginia, the two Carolinas, Georgia, Alabama, fall under their power, what then? Will they be masters of a country they can never occupy? No, certainly not; and for my part, if they are ever victorious, they shall pay dearly for it."

"And you are quite sure of your soldiers?" asked the Captain. "You are not afraid that Charleston will grow weary of a siege which is ruining her?"

"No, I do not fear treason; besides, the traitors would be punished remorselessly, and I would destroy the town itself by sword or fire if I discovered the least Unionist movement. Jefferson Davis confided Charleston to me, and you may be sure that Charleston is in safe hands."

"Have you any Federal prisoners?" asked James Playfair, coming to the interesting object of the conversation.

"Yes, Captain," replied the General, "it was at Charleston that the first shot of separation was fired. The Abolitionists who were here attempted to resist, and, after being defeated, they have been kept as prisoners of war."

"And have you many?"

"About a hundred."

"Free in the town?"

"They were until I discovered a plot formed by them: their chief succeeded in establishing a communication with the besiegers, who were thus informed of the situation of affairs in the town. I was then obliged to lock up these dangerous guests, and several of them will only leave their prison to ascend the slope of the citadel, where ten confederate balls will reward them for their federalism."

"What! to be shot!" cried the young man, shuddering involuntarily.

"Yes, and their chief first of all. He is a very dangerous man to have in a besieged town. I have sent his letters to the President at Richmond, and before a week is passed his sentence will be irrevocably passed."

"Who is this man you speak of?" asked James Playfair, with an assumed carelessness.

"A journalist from Boston, a violent Abolitionist with the confounded spirit of Lincoln."

"And his name?"

"Jonathan Halliburtt."

"Poor wretch!" exclaimed James, suppressing his emotion. "Whatever he may have done, one cannot help pitying him. And you think that he will be shot?"

"I am sure of it," replied Beauregard. "What can you expect? War is war; one must defend oneself as best one can."

"Well, it is nothing to me," said the Captain. "I shall be far enough away when this execution takes place."

"What! you are thinking of going away already."

"Yes, General, business must be attended to; as soon as my cargo of cotton is on board I shall be out to sea again. I was fortunate enough to enter the bay, but the difficulty is in getting out again. The Dolphin is a good ship;

she can beat any of the Federal vessels for speed, but she does not pretend to distance cannon-balls, and a shell in her hull or engine would seriously affect my enterprise."

"As you please, Captain," replied Beauregard; "I have no advice to give you under such circumstances. You are doing your business, and you are right. I should act in the same manner were I in your place; besides, a stay at Charleston is not very pleasant, and a harbour where shells are falling three days out of four is not a safe shelter for your ship; so you will set sail when you please; but can you tell me what is the number and the force of the Federal vessels cruising before Charleston?"

James Playfair did his best to answer the General, and took leave of him on the best of terms; then he returned to the Dolphin very thoughtful and very depressed from what he had just heard.

"What shall I say to Miss Jenny? Ought I to tell her of Mr. Halliburtt's terrible situation? Or would it be better to keep her in ignorance of the trial which is awaiting her? Poor child!"

He had not gone fifty steps from the governor's house when he ran against Crockston. The worthy American had been watching for him since his departure.

"Well, Captain?"

James Playfair looked steadily at Crockston, and the latter soon understood he had no favourable news to give him.

"Have you seen Beauregard?" he asked.

"Yes," replied James Playfair.

"And have you spoken to him about Mr. Halliburtt?"

"No, it was he who spoke to me about him."

"Well, Captain?"

"Well, I may as well tell you everything, Crockston."

"Everything, Captain."

"General Beauregard has told me that your master will be shot within a week."

At this news anyone else but Crockston would have grown furious or given way to bursts of grief, but the American, who feared nothing, only said, with almost a smile on his lips:

"Pooh! what does it matter?"

"How! what does it matter?" cried James Playfair. "I tell you that Mr. Halliburtt will be shot within a week, and you answer, what does it matter?"

"And I mean it—if in six days he is on board the Dolphin, and if in seven days the Dolphin is on the open sea."

"Right!" exclaimed the Captain, pressing Crockston's hand. "I understand, my good fellow, you have got some pluck; and for myself, in spite of Uncle Vincent, I would throw myself overboard for Miss Jenny."

"No one need be thrown overboard," replied the American, "only the fish would gain by that: the most important business now is to deliver Mr. Halliburtt."

"But you must know that it will be difficult to do so."

"Pooh!" exclaimed Crockston.

"It is a question of communicating with a prisoner strictly guarded."

"Certainly."

"And to bring about an almost miraculous escape."

"Nonsense," exclaimed Crockston; "a prisoner thinks more of escaping than his guardian thinks of keeping him; that's why, thanks to our help, Mr. Halliburtt will be saved."

"You are right, Crockston."

"Always right."

"But now what will you do? There must be some plan: and there are precautions to be taken."

"I will think about it."

"But when Miss Jenny learns that her father is condemned to death, and that the order for his execution may come any day—"

"She will know nothing about it, that is all."

"Yes, it will be better for her and for us to tell her nothing."

"Where is Mr. Halliburtt imprisoned?" asked Crockston.

"In the citadel," replied James Playfair.

"Just so! . . . On board now?"

"On board, Crockston!"

THE ESCAPE

Miss Jenny, sitting at the poop of the Dolphin, was anxiously waiting the Captain's return; when the latter went up to her she could not utter a word, but her eyes questioned James Playfair more eagerly than her lips could have done. The latter, with Crockston's help, informed the young girl of the facts relating to her father's imprisonment. He said that he had carefully broached the subject of the prisoners of war to Beauregard, but, as the General did not seem disposed at all in their favour, he had thought it better to say no more about it, but think the matter over again.

"Since Mr. Halliburtt is not free in the town, his escape will be more difficult; but I will finish my task, and I promise you, Miss Jenny, that the Dolphin shall not leave Charleston without having your father on board."

"Thank you, Mr. James; I thank you with my whole heart."

At these words James Playfair felt a thrill of joy through his whole being.

He approached the young girl with moist eyes and quivering lips; perhaps he was going to make an avowal of the sentiments he could no longer repress, when Crockston interfered:

"This is no time for grieving," said he; "we must go to work, and consider what to do."

"Have you any plan, Crockston?" asked the young girl.

"I always have a plan," replied the American: "it is my peculiarity."

"But a good one?" said James Playfair.

"Excellent! and all the ministers in Washington could not devise a better; it is almost as good as if Mr. Halliburtt was already on board."

Crockston spoke with such perfect assurance, at the same time with such simplicity, that it must have been the most incredulous person who could doubt his words.

"We are listening, Crockston," said James Playfair.

"Good! You, Captain, will go to General Beauregard, and ask a favour of him which he will not refuse you."

"And what is that?"

"You will tell him that you have on board a tiresome subject, a scamp who has been very troublesome during the voyage, and excited the crew to revolt. You will ask of him permission to shut him up in the citadel; at the same time, on the condition that he shall return to the ship on her departure, in order to be taken back to England, to be delivered over to the justice of his country."

"Good!" said James Playfair, half smiling, "I will do all that, and Beauregard will grant my request very willingly."

"I am perfectly sure of it," replied the American.

"But," resumed Playfair, "one thing is wanting."

"What is that?"

"The scamp."

"He is before you, Captain."

"What, the rebellious subject?"

"Is myself; don't trouble yourself about that."

"Oh! you brave, generous heart," cried Jenny, pressing the American's rough hands between her small white palms.

"Go, Crockston," said James Playfair; "I understand you, my friend; and I only regret one thing—that is, that I cannot take your place."

"Everyone his part," replied Crockston; "if you put yourself in my place you would be very much embarrassed, which I shall not be; you will have enough to do later on to get out of the harbour under the fire of the Feds and Rebs, which, for my part, I should manage very badly."

"Well, Crockston, go on."

"Once in the citadel—I know it—I shall see what to do, and rest assured I shall do my best; in the meanwhile, you will be getting your cargo on board."

"Oh, business is now a very unimportant detail," said the Captain.

"Not at all! And what would your Uncle Vincent say to that? We must join sentiment with work; it will prevent suspicion; but do it quickly. Can you be ready in six days?"

"Yes."

"Well, let the Dolphin be ready to start on the 22nd."

"She shall be ready."

"On the evening of the 22nd of January, you understand, send a gig with your best men to White Point, at the end of the town; wait there till nine o'clock, and then you will see Mr. Halliburtt and your servant."

"But how will you manage to effect Mr. Halliburtt's deliverance, and also escape yourself?"

"That's my look-out."

"Dear Crockston, you are going to risk your life then, to save my father!"

"Don't be uneasy, Miss Jenny, I shall risk absolutely nothing, you may believe me."

"Well," asked James Playfair, "when must I have you locked up?"

"To-day—you understand—I demoralise your crew; there is no time to be lost."

"Would you like any money? It may be of use to you in the citadel."

"Money to buy the gaoler! Oh, no, it would be a poor bargain; when one goes there the gaoler keeps the money and the prisoner! No, I have surer means than that; however, a few dollars may be useful; one must be able to drink, if needs be."

"And intoxicate the gaoler."

"No, an intoxicated gaoler would spoil everything. No, I tell you I have an idea; let me work it out."

"Here, my good fellow, are ten dollars."

"It is too much, but I will return what is over."

"Well, then, are you ready?"

"Quite ready to be a downright rogue."

"Let us go to work, then."

"Crockston," said the young girl, in a faltering voice, "you are the best man on earth."

"I know it," replied the American, laughing good-humouredly. "By the by, Captain, an important item."

"What is that?"

"If the General proposes to hang your rebel—you know that military men like sharp work—"

"Well, Crockston?"

"Well, you will say that you must think about it."

"I promise you I will."

The same day, to the great astonishment of the crew, who were not in the secret, Crockston, with his feet and hands in irons, was taken on shore by a dozen sailors, and half an hour after, by Captain James Playfair's request, he was led through the streets of the town, and, in spite of his resistance, was imprisoned in the citadel.

During this and the following days the unloading of the Dolphin was rapidly accomplished; the steam cranes lifted out the European cargo to make room for the native goods. The people of Charleston, who were present at this interesting work, helped the sailors, whom they held in great respect, but the Captain did not leave the brave fellows much time for receiving compliments; he was constantly behind them, and urged them on with a feverish activity, the reason of which the sailors could not suspect.

Three days later, on the 18th of January, the first bales of cotton began to be packed in the hold: although James Playfair troubled himself no more about it, the firm of Playfair and Co. were making an excellent bargain, having obtained the cotton which encumbered the Charleston wharves at very far less than its value.

In the meantime no news had been heard of Crockston. Jenny, without saying anything about it, was a prey to incessant fears; her pale face spoke for her, and James Playfair endeavoured his utmost to ease her mind.

"I have all confidence in Crockston," said he; "he is a devoted servant, as you must know better than I do, Miss Jenny. You must make yourself quite at ease; believe me, in three days you will be folded in your father's arms."

"Ah! Mr. James," cried the young girl, "how can I ever repay you for such devotion? How shall we ever be able to thank you?"

"I will tell you when we are in English seas," replied the young Captain.

Jenny raised her tearful face to him for a moment, then her eyelids drooped, and she went back to her cabin.

James Playfair hoped that the young girl would know nothing of her father's terrible situation until he was in safety, but she was apprised of the truth by the involuntary indiscretion of a sailor.

The reply from the Richmond cabinet had arrived by a courier who had been able to pass the line of outposts; the reply contained Jonathan Halliburtt's death-warrant. The news of the approaching execution was not long in spreading through the town, and it was brought on board by one of the sailors of the Dolphin; the man told the Captain, without thinking that Miss Halliburtt was within hearing; the young girl uttered a piercing cry, and fell unconscious on the deck. James Playfair carried her to her cabin, but the most assiduous care was necessary to restore her to life.

When she opened her eyes again, she saw the young Captain, who, with a finger on his lips, enjoined absolute silence. With difficulty she repressed the outburst of her grief, and James Playfair, leaning towards her, said gently:

"Jenny, in two hours your father will be in safety near you, or I shall have perished in endeavouring to save him!"

Then he left the cabin, saying to himself, "And now he must be carried off at any price, since I must pay for his liberty with my own life and those of my crew."

The hour for action had arrived, the loading of the cotton cargo had been finished since morning; in two hours the ship would be ready to start.

James Playfair had left the North Commercial Wharf and gone into the roadstead, so that he was ready to make use of the tide, which would be high at nine o'clock in the evening.

It was seven o'clock when James left the young girl, and began to make preparations for departure. Until the present time the secret had been strictly kept between himself, Crockston, and Jenny; but now he thought it wise to inform Mr. Mathew of the situation of affairs, and he did so immediately.

"Very well, sir," replied Mr. Mathew, without making the least remark, "and nine o'clock is the time?"

"Nine o'clock, and have the fires lit immediately, and the steam got up."

"It shall be done, Captain."

"The Dolphin may remain at anchor; we will cut our moorings and sheer off, without losing a moment."

"Just so."

"Have a lantern placed at the mainmast-head; the night is dark, and will be foggy; we must not risk losing our way in returning. You had better have the bell for starting rung at nine o'clock."

"Your orders shall be punctually attended to, Captain."

"And now, Mr. Mathew, have a shore-boat manned with six of our best men. I am going to set out directly for White Point. I leave Miss Jenny in your charge, and may God protect us!"

"May God protect us!" repeated the first officer.

Then he immediately gave the necessary orders for the fires to be lighted, and the shore-boat provided with men. In a few minutes the boat was ready, and James Playfair, after bidding Jenny good-bye, stepped into it, whilst at the same time he saw volumes of black smoke issuing from the chimneys of the ship, and losing itself in the fog.

The darkness was profound; the wind had fallen, and in the perfect silence the waters seemed to slumber in the immense harbour, whilst a few uncertain lights glimmered through the mist. James Playfair had taken his place at the rudder, and with a steady hand he guided his boat towards White Point. It was a distance of about two miles; during the day James had taken his bearings perfectly, so that he was able to make direct for Charleston Point.

Eight o'clock struck from the church of St. Philip when the shore-boat ran aground at White Point.

There was an hour to wait before the exact time fixed by Crockston; the quay was deserted, with the exception of the sentinel pacing to and fro on the south and east batteries. James Playfair grew impatient, and the minutes seemed hours to him.

At half-past eight he heard the sound of approaching steps; he left his men with their oars clear and ready to start, and went himself to see who it was; but he had not gone ten feet when he met a band of coastguards, in all about twenty men. James drew his revolver from his waist, deciding to make use of it, if needs be; but what could he do against these soldiers, who were coming on to the quay?

The leader came up to him, and, seeing the boat, asked:

"Whose craft is that?"

"It is a gig belonging to the Dolphin," replied the young man.

"And who are you?"

"Captain James Playfair."

"I thought you had already started, and were now in the Charleston channels."

"I am ready to start. I ought even now to be on my way but—"

"But—" persisted the coastguard.

A bright idea shot through James's mind, and he answered:

"One of my sailors is locked up in the citadel, and, to tell the truth, I had almost forgotten him; fortunately I thought of him in time, and I have sent my men to bring him."

"Ah! that troublesome fellow; you wish to take him back to England?"

"Yes.

"He might as well be hung here as there," said the coast-guard, laughing at his joke.

"So I think," said James Playfair, "but it is better to have the thing done in the regular way."

"Not much chance of that, Captain, when you have to face the Morris Island batteries."

"Don't alarm yourself. I got in and I'll get out again."

"Prosperous voyage to you!"

"Thank you."

With this the men went off, and the shore was left silent.

At this moment nine o'clock struck; it was the appointed moment. James felt his heart beat violently; a whistle was heard; he replied to it, then he waited, listening, with his hand up to enjoin perfect silence on the sailors. A man appeared enveloped in a large cloak, and looking from one side to another. James ran up to him.

"Mr. Halliburtt?"

"I am he," replied the man with the cloak.

"God be praised!" cried James Playfair. "Embark without losing a minute. Where is Crockston?"

"Crockston!" exclaimed Mr. Halliburtt, amazed. "What do you mean?"

"The man who has saved you and brought you here was your servant Crockston."

"The man who came with me was the gaoler from the citadel," replied Mr. Halliburtt.

"The gaoler!" cried James Playfair.

Evidently he knew nothing about it, and a thousand fears crowded in his mind.

"Quite right, the gaoler," cried a well-known voice. "The gaoler is sleeping like a top in my cell."

"Crockston! you! Can it be you?" exclaimed Mr. Halliburtt.

"No time to talk now, master; we will explain everything to you afterwards. It is a question of life or death. Get in quick!"

The three men took their places in the boat.

"Push off!" cried the captain.

Immediately the six oars dipped into the water; the boat darted like a fish through the waters of Charleston Harbour.

BETWEEN TWO FIRES

The boat, pulled by six robust oarsmen, flew over the water. The fog was growing dense, and it was with difficulty that James Playfair succeeded in keeping to the line of his bearings. Crockston sat at the bows, and Mr. Halliburtt at the stern, next the Captain. The prisoner, only now informed of the presence of his servant, wished to speak to him, but the latter enjoined silence.

However, a few minutes later, when they were in the middle of the harbour, Crockston determined to speak, knowing what thoughts were uppermost in Mr. Halliburtt's mind.

"Yes, my dear master," said he, "the gaoler is in my place in the cell, where I gave him two smart blows, one on the head and the other on the stomach, to act as a sleeping draught, and this when he was bringing me my supper; there is gratitude for you. I took his clothes and his keys, found you, and let you out of the citadel, under the soldiers' noses. That is all I have done."

"But my daughter—?" asked Mr. Halliburtt.

"Is on board the ship which is going to take you to England."

"My daughter there! there!" cried the American, springing from his seat.

"Silence!" replied Crockston, "a few minutes, and we shall be saved."

The boat flew through the darkness, but James Playfair was obliged to steer rather by guess, as the lanterns of the Dolphin were no longer visible through the fog. He was undecided what direction to follow, and the darkness was so great that the rowers could not even see to the end of their oars.

"Well, Mr. James?" said Crockston.

"We must have made more than a mile and a half," replied the Captain. "You don't see anything, Crockston?"

"Nothing; nevertheless, I have good eyes; but we shall get there all right. They don't suspect anything out there."

These words were hardly finished when the flash of a gun gleamed for an instant through the darkness, and vanished in the mist.

"A signal!" cried James Playfair.

"Whew!" exclaimed Crockston. "It must have come from the citadel. Let us wait."

A second, then a third shot was fired in the direction of the first, and almost the same signal was repeated a mile in front of the gig.

"That is from Fort Sumter," cried Crockston, "and it is the signal of escape. Urge on the men; everything is discovered."

"Pull for your lives, my men!" cried James Playfair, urging on the sailors, "those gun-shots cleared my route. The Dolphin is eight hundred yards ahead of us. Stop! I hear the bell on board. Hurrah, there it is again! Twenty pounds for you if we are back in five minutes!"

The boat skimmed over the waves under the sailors' powerful oars. A cannon boomed in the direction of the town. Crockston heard a ball whiz past them.

The bell on the Dolphin was ringing loudly. A few more strokes and the boat was alongside. A few more seconds and Jenny fell into her father's arms.

The gig was immediately raised, and James Playfair sprang on to the poop.

"Is the steam up, Mr. Mathew?"

"Yes, Captain."

"Have the moorings cut at once."

A few minutes later the two screws carried the steamer towards the principal channel, away from Fort Sumter.

"Mr. Mathew," said James, "we must not think of taking the Sullivan Island channel; we should run directly under the Confederate guns. Let us go as near as possible to the right side of the harbour out of range of the Federal batteries. Have you a safe man at the helm?"

"Yes, Captain."

"Have the lanterns and the fires on deck extinguished; there is a great deal too much light, but we cannot help the reflection from the engine-rooms."

During this conversation the Dolphin was going at a great speed; but in altering her course to keep to the right side of the Charleston Harbour she was obliged to enter a channel which took her for a moment near Fort Sumter; and when scarcely half a mile off all the guns bearing on her were discharged at the same time, and a shower of shot and shell passed in front of the Dolphin with a thundering report.

"Too soon, stupids," cried James Playfair, with a burst of laughter. "Make haste, make haste, Mr. Engineer! We shall get between two fires."

The stokers fed the furnaces, and the Dolphin trembled all over with the effort of the engine as if she was on the point of exploding.

At this moment a second report was heard, and another shower of balls whizzed behind the Dolphin.

"Too late, stupids," cried the young Captain, with a regular roar.

Then Crockston, who was standing on the poop, cried, "That's one passed. A few minutes more, and we shall have done with the Rebs."

"Then do you think we have nothing more to fear from Fort Sumter?" asked James.

"Nothing at all, but everything from Fort Moultrie, at the end of Sullivan Island; but they will only get a chance at us for half a minute, and then they must choose their time well, and shoot straight if they want to reach us. We are getting near."

"Right; the position of Fort Moultrie will allow us to go straight for the principal channel. Fire away then, fire away!"

At the same moment, and as if in obedience to James Playfair, the fort was illuminated by a triple line of lightning. A frightful crash was heard; then a crackling sound on board the steamer.

"Touched this time!" exclaimed Crockston.

"Mr. Mathew!" cried the Captain to his second, who was stationed at the bows, "what has been damaged?"

"The bowsprit broken."

"Any wounded?"

"No, Captain."

"Well, then, the masts may go to Jericho. Straight into the pass! Straight! and steer towards the island."

"We have passed the Rebs!" cried Crockston; "and, if we must have balls in our hull, I would much rather have the Northerners; they are more easily digested."

In fact, the Dolphin could not yet consider herself out of danger; for, if Morris Island was not fortified with the formidable pieces of artillery which were placed there a few months later, nevertheless its guns and mortars could easily have sunk a ship like the Dolphin.

The alarm had been given to the Federals on the island, and to the blockading squadron, by the firing from Forts Sumter and Moultrie. The besiegers could not make out the reason of this night attack; it did not seem to be directed against them. However, they were obliged to consider it so, and were ready to reply.

It occupied James Playfair's thoughts whilst making towards the passes of Morris Island; and he had reason to fear, for in a quarter of an hour's time lights gleamed rapidly through the darkness. A shower of small shell fell round the steamer, scattering the water over her bulwarks; some of them even struck the deck of the Dolphin, but not on their points, which saved the ship from certain ruin. In fact, these shell, as it was afterwards discovered, could break into a hundred fragments, and each cover a superficial area of a hundred and twenty square feet with Greek fire, which would burn for twenty minutes, and nothing could extinguish it. One of these shell alone could set a ship on fire. Fortunately for the Dolphin, they were a new invention, and as yet far from perfect. Once thrown into the air, a false rotary movement kept them inclined, and, when falling, instead of striking on their points, where is the percussion apparatus, they fell flat. This defect in construction alone saved the Dolphin. The falling of these shells did her little harm, and under the pressure of her over-heated boilers she continued to advance into the pass.

At this moment, and in spite of his orders, Mr. Halliburtt and his daughter went to James Playfair on the poop; the latter urged them to return to their cabins, but Jenny declared that she would remain by the Captain. As for Mr. Halliburtt, who had just learnt all the noble conduct of his deliverer, he pressed his hand without being able to utter a word.

The Dolphin was speeding rapidly towards the open sea. There were only three miles more before she would be in the waters of the Atlantic; if the pass was free at its entrance, she was saved. James Playfair was wonderfully well acquainted with all the secrets of Charleston Bay, and he guided his ship through the darkness with an unerring hand. He was beginning to think his daring enterprise successful, when a sailor on the forecastle cried:

"A ship!"

"A ship?" cried James.

"Yes, on the larboard side."

The fog had cleared off, and a large frigate was seen making towards the pass, in order to obstruct the passage of the Dolphin. It was necessary, cost what it might, to distance her, and urge the steam-engine to an increase of speed, or all was lost.

"Port the helm at once!" cried the Captain.

Then he sprang on to the bridge above the engine. By his orders one of the screws was stopped, and under the action of the other the Dolphin, veering with an extraordinary rapidity, avoided running foul of the frigate, and advanced like her to the entrance of the pass. It was now a question of speed.

James Playfair understood that in this lay his own safety, Miss Jenny's, her father's, and that of all his crew.

The frigate was considerably in advance of the Dolphin. It was evident from the volumes of black smoke issuing from her chimneys that she was getting up her steam. James Playfair was not the man to be left in the background.

"How are the engines?" cried he to the engineer.

"At the maximum speed," replied the latter; "the steam is escaping by all the valves."

"Fasten them down," ordered the Captain.

And his orders were executed at the risk of blowing up the ship.

The Dolphin again increased her speed; the pistons worked with frightful rapidity; the metal plates on which the engine was placed trembled under the terrific force of their blows. It was a sight to make the boldest shudder.

"More pressure!" cried James Playfair; "put on more pressure!"

"Impossible!" replied the engineer. "The valves are tightly closed; our furnaces are full up to the mouths."

"What difference! Fill them with cotton soaked in spirits; we must pass that frigate at any price."

At these words the most daring of the sailors looked at each other, but did not hesitate. Some bales of cotton were thrown into the engine-room, a barrel of spirits broached over them, and this expensive fuel placed, not without danger, in the red-hot furnaces. The stokers could no longer hear each other speak for the roaring of the flames. Soon the metal plates of the furnaces became red-hot; the pistons worked like the pistons of a locomotive; the steamgauge showed a frightful tension; the steamer flew over the water; her boards creaked, and her chimneys threw out volumes of smoke mingled with flames. She was going at a headlong speed, but, nevertheless, she was gaining on the frigate—passed her, distanced her, and in ten minutes was out of the channel.

"Saved!" cried the Captain.

"Saved!" echoed the crew, clapping their hands.

Already the Charleston beacon was disappearing in the south-west; the sound of firing from the batteries grew fainter, and it might with reason be thought that the danger was all past, when a shell from a gun-boat cruising at large was hurled whizzing through the air. It was easy to trace its course, thanks to the line of fire which followed it.

Then was a moment of anxiety impossible to describe; every one was silent, and each watched fearfully the arch described by the projectile. Nothing could be done to escape it, and in a few seconds it fell with a frightful noise on the fore-deck of the Dolphin.

The terrified sailors crowded to the stern, and no one dared move a step, whilst the shell was burning with a brisk crackle.

But one brave man alone among them ran up to the formidable weapon of destruction. It was Crockston; he took the shell in his strong arms, whilst showers of sparks were falling from it; then, with a superhuman effort, he threw it overboard.

Hardly had the shell reached the surface of the water when it burst with a frightful report.

"Hurrah! hurrah!" cried the whole crew of the Dolphin unanimously, whilst Crockston rubbed his hands.

Some time later the steamer sped rapidly through the waters of the Atlantic; the American coast disappeared in the darkness, and the distant lights which shot across the horizon indicated that the attack was general between the batteries of Morris Island and the forts of Charleston Harbour.

ST. MUNGO

The next day at sunrise the American coast had disappeared; not a ship was visible on the horizon, and the Dolphin, moderating the frightful rapidity of her speed, made quietly towards the Bermudas.

It is useless to recount the passage across the Atlantic, which was marked by no accidents, and ten days after the departure from Queenstown the French coast was hailed.

What passed between the Captain and the young girl may be imagined, even by the least observant individuals. How could Mr. Halliburtt acknowledge the devotion and courage of his deliverer, if it was not by making him the happiest of men? James Playfair did not wait for English seas to declare to the father and daughter the sentiments which overflowed his heart, and, if Crockston is to be believed, Miss Jenny received his confession with a happiness she did not try to conceal.

Thus it happened that on the 14th of February, 18—, a numerous crowd was collected in the dim aisles of St. Mungo, the old cathedral of Glasgow. There were seamen, merchants, manufacturers, magistrates, and some of every denomination gathered here. There was Miss Jenny in bridal array and beside her the worthy Crockston, resplendent in apple-green clothes, with gold buttons, whilst Uncle Vincent stood proudly by his nephew.

In short, they were celebrating the marriage of James Playfair, of the firm of Vincent Playfair & Co., of Glasgow, with Miss Jenny Halliburtt, of Boston.

The ceremony was accomplished amidst great pomp. Everyone knew the history of the Dolphin, and everyone thought the young Captain well recompensed for his devotion. He alone said that his reward was greater than he deserved.

In the evening there was a grand ball and banquet at Uncle Vincent's house, with a large distribution of shillings to the crowd collected in Gordon Street. Crockston did ample justice to this memorable feast, while keeping himself perfectly within bounds.

Everyone was happy at this wedding; some at their own happiness, and others at the happiness around them, which is not always the case at ceremonies of this kind.

Late in the evening, when the guests had retired, James Playfair took his uncle's hand.

"Well, Uncle Vincent," said he to him.

"Well, Nephew James?"

"Are you pleased with the charming cargo I brought you on board the Dolphin?" continued Captain Playfair, showing him his brave young wife.

"I am quite satisfied," replied the worthy merchant; "I have sold my cotton at three hundred and seventy-five per cent. profit."

www.ingramcontent.com/pod-product-compliance
Lightning Source LLC
Chambersburg PA
CBHW021226020426
42331CB00003B/489

9 7 9 8 8 8 0 9 1 3 4 3 5